I Feel...
SICK

Words and pictures by

DJ Corchin

sourcebooks
eXplore

Sometimes I feel **sick.**

Sometimes my **head aches.**

Sometimes my nose **runs**...

...all over my face.

Sometimes I don't feel well and my tummy's **upset**...

...'Cause I ate too much chocolate,

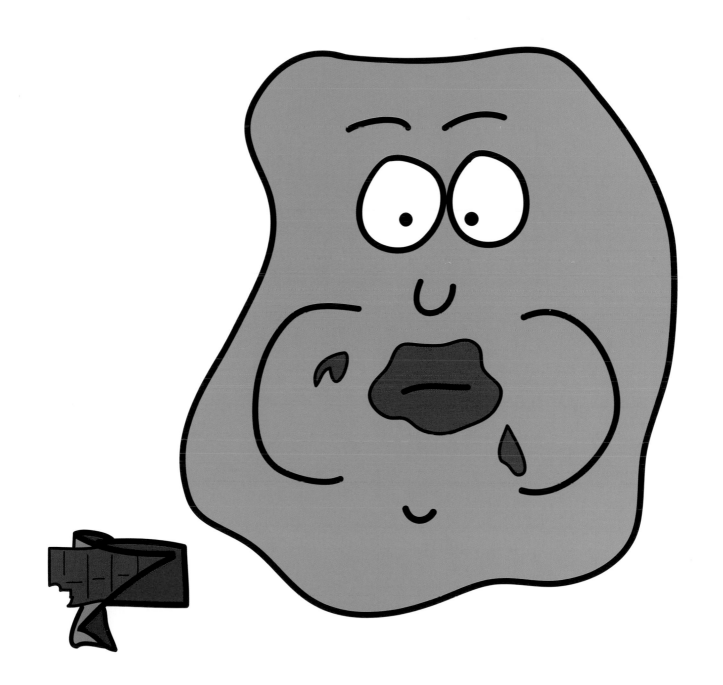

which I **completely regret...**

...and now I've come down
with the chocolaty sweats.

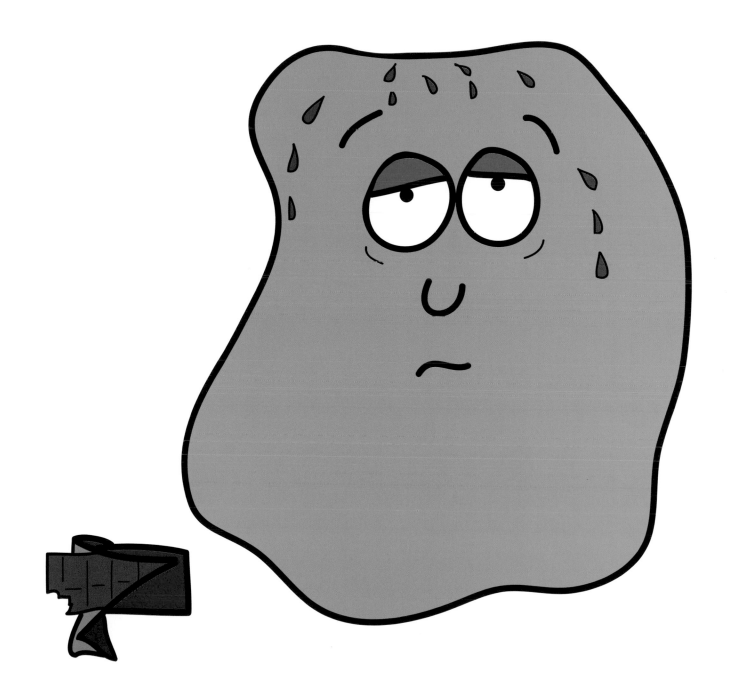

Sometimes I feel **tired**

or have a **rash** on my skin.

Sometimes I get **dizzy**
and the room starts to spin.

Sometimes I am **cold.**

Sometimes I am **hot.**

Sometimes I am **both**...

...then **throw up** in a pot.

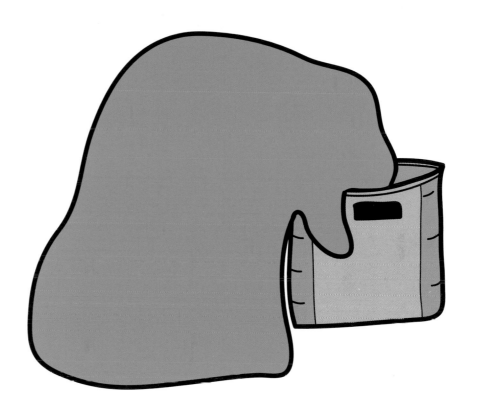

My doctor's not sure
which **bug** that I got.

So he takes a small **swab**...

...of what seems to be **snot**.

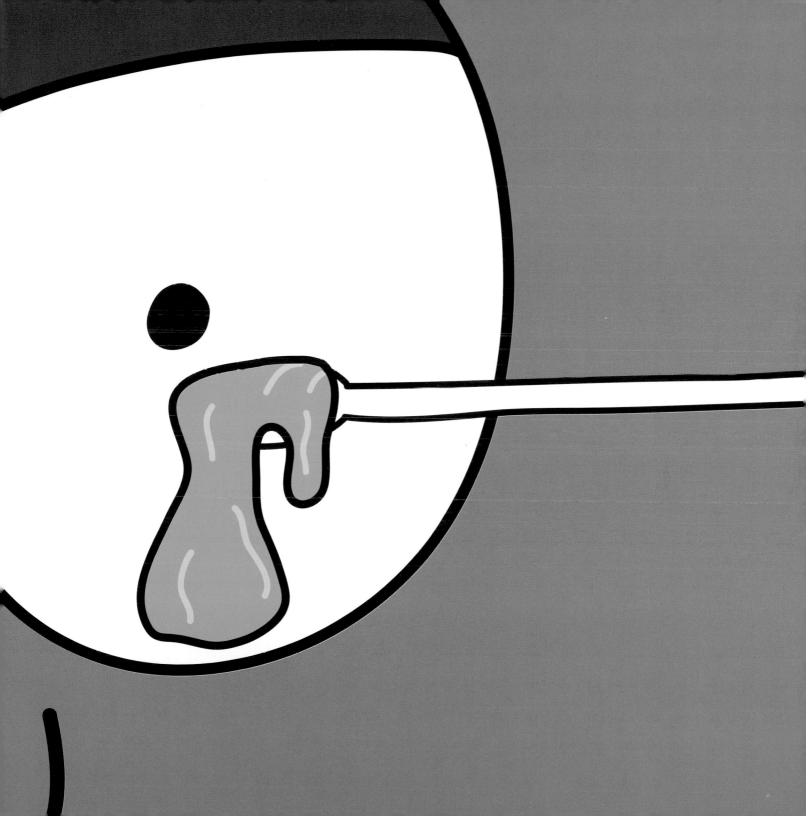

Sometimes I am **gassy.**

And the room starts to **stink.**

Or my eyes get all **puffy** and **itchy** and **pink.**

My throat gets quite **sore** so it hurts when I drink.

But the medicine is **grape**...
at least flavored I think.

Sometimes I'm quite ill, and it's really **not fun**...

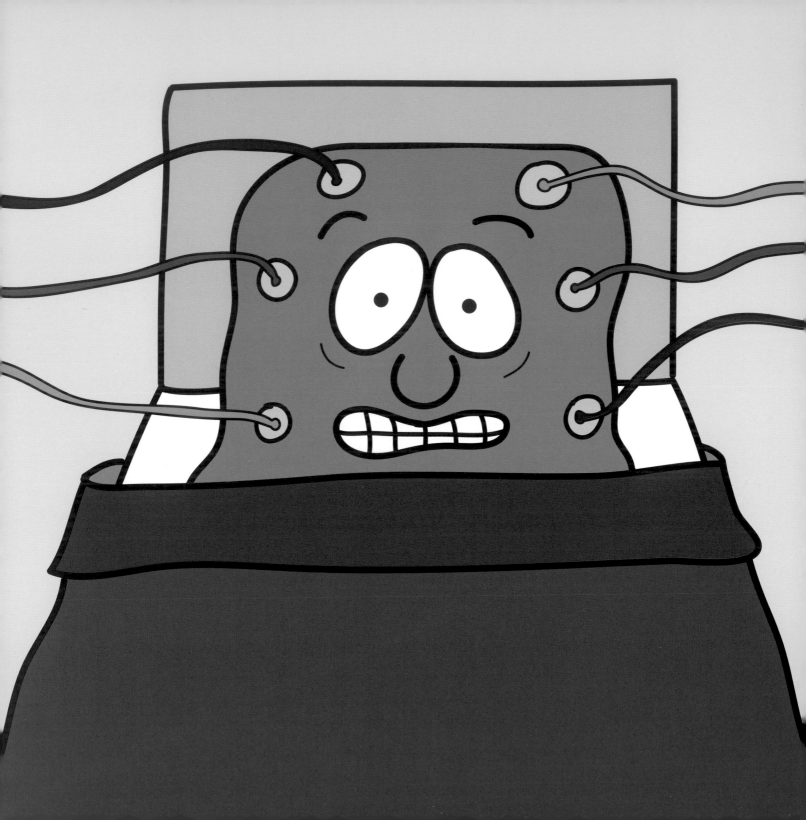

...to visit a **hospital** for tests to be run.

But I'll be better soon,
and back to my **tricks**.

'Cause I have people who **love me**, even when I feel sick.

I Feel...
SICK

Sometimes you get sick. It's important to get rest and know that people care about you.

It happens. Sometimes you don't feel well. Sometimes it's a simple stuffy nose and you just have to get some sleep. Sometimes it's a bit more and you're stuck in your room for a while. Being sick is never fun, but there are activities you can do to pass the time and keep your spirits up.

Make an I Feel... Sick Ready Kit

When you're feeling well, create a kit so you're ready with things to do when you might feel ill.

1. Find a box big enough to fit a basketball in.

2. Write on the top, I Feel... Sick Ready Kit.

3. Add different types of paper (construction paper, recycled white paper, colorful sticky notes, etc.)

4. Add one pack of washable markers, one pack of crayons, one pack of colored pencils, and any other drawing tools you like. You can place them in different small bags (cloth if possible) or containers to keep them from rolling around.

5. Add scissors and stencils.

6. Add glue (glitter glue if possible.)

7. Add a small sketchbook.

8. Add some playing cards or your favorite card game.

9. Add a coloring book or two.

10. Add a couple books that you haven't read yet.

Cozy Corner

1. Grab a few warm blankets and pillows.

2. Find a quiet corner in your home or room.

3. Fill it with blankets, pillows, and stuffed animals.

4. Add your favorite book and a flashlight or lamp.

5. You can decorate the corner with pictures or art.

It is ALWAYS OK to ask someone for help when you are feeling bad.

The I Feel... Children's Series is a resource created to assist in discussions about emotional awareness.

Please seek the help of a trained mental healthcare professional and start a discussion today.

6. Use this corner to rest, read a book, draw a picture, and more. If you pick a cozy corner near a TV, maybe you can watch your favorite movie or show!

Let's Try Something New

Sometimes people discover new talents and passions while sick because they have some time to try something new while resting. The author of this book wrote the first I Feel... book while sick in bed!

1. Make a list of some things you want to try or learn if you had the time. Some examples: Write a poem, learn a language, learn to draw, write a book, etc.

2. Cut 1-inch thick strips about the width of an 8.5 x 11 piece of paper.

3. Write down your ideas on the strips of paper. One idea for each strip.

4. Crumple them up and put them in a bowl.

5. On a day when you're home sick resting, pick a strip from the bowl.

6. Have fun exploring something new!

My I Feel... Sick Journal

Feeling sick can be exhausting and not very fun. In times like these, it's important to still talk about your feelings.

1. Grab ten pieces of recycled white or notebook paper. With all of them stacked together, folder them in half, creating a book. You can staple the pages in the middle to keep them together. (You can also use a pre-made notebook if you have one!)

2. On the cover, draw an I Feel... face that expresses how you're currently feeling and write "My I Feel... Sick Journal" as the title.

3. On each page at the top, write the date.

4. Write a short paragraph about what you're feeling in your body as well as what emotions you have.

5. You can draw pictures about how you feel instead of writing if that is more fun for you.

6. Each day, take some time to think about how you're feeling and if you need something from an adult.

Art Gallery

1. Choose four different themes such as Sky, Water, Magic, and Animals.

2. Pick a theme for each of the four walls in your room.

3. Using your I Feel... Sick Ready Kit or spare art supplies, create different types of drawings about each theme.

4. Create a sign for each wall with the name of the theme.

5. Hang or tape up all the drawings on each wall.

6. If it's OK, invite family members in to see your art gallery.

7. You can share your art gallery through a video call on your phone, tablet, or computer.

To Ann

Published by Sourcebooks eXplore, an imprint of Sourcebooks Kids
P.O. Box 4410, Naperville, Illinois 60567-4410
(630) 961-3900
sourcebookskids.com

Originally published in 2012 in the United States of America by The phazelFOZ Company, LLC.

Library of Congress Cataloging-in-Publication Data is on file with the publisher.

Source of Production: 1010 Printing Asia Limited, North Point, Hong Kong, China
Date of Production: July 2020
Run Number: 5019240

Printed and bound in China.
OGP 10 9 8 7 6 5 4 3 2 1